SHIPS AHOY!

Submarines

by Kaitlyn Duling

BLASTOFF! READERS 2

BLASTOFF! READERS, AN IMPRINT OF BELLWETHER MEDIA BY FLUTTERBEE

Blastoff! Readers are carefully developed by literacy experts to build reading stamina and move students toward fluency by combining standards-based content with developmentally appropriate text.

Level 1 provides the most support through repetition of high-frequency words, light text, predictable sentence patterns, and strong visual support.

Level 2 offers early readers a bit more challenge through varied sentences, increased text load, and text-supportive special features.

Level 3 advances early-fluent readers toward fluency through increased text load, less reliance on photos, advancing concepts, longer sentences, and more complex special features.

★ Blastoff! Universe

Reading Level

Grade K → Grades 1–3 → Grade 4

This edition first published in 2026 by Bellwether Media, Inc.

Library of Congress Cataloging-in-Publication Data is available at www.loc.gov or upon request from the publisher.

ISBN: 9798893048025 (hardcover)
ISBN: 9798893049022 (ebook)

Editor: Kieran Downs Designer: Jennifer Bowyer

Printed in the United States of America, North Mankato, MN.

Table of Contents

What Are Submarines?

Submarines travel above and below water. They are often called subs.

Subs can be very big
or very small.

Subs are usually shaped like a teardrop.

The **sail** sticks out of the water. A **periscope** on the sail helps the crew see above water.

Parts of a Submarine

Many subs have a **nuclear reactor** in the **engine** room.

The reactor creates **steam**. The steam helps turn a **propeller**. This makes the sub move!

engine room

Attack subs are used
by armed forces.
They carry weapons.

Types of Submarines

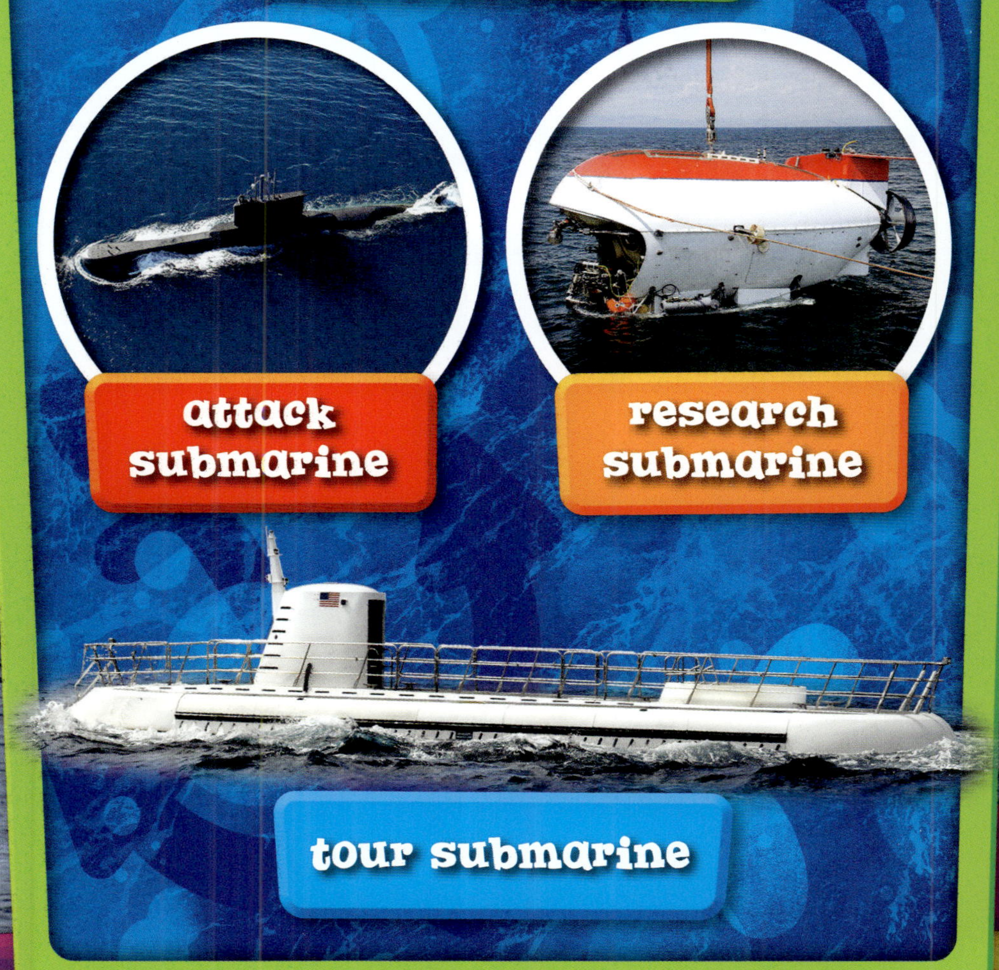

Research subs are used by scientists. Visitors go underwater in **tour** subs.

Deep Dive

Subs can have more than one hundred crew members.

The **quartermaster** helps control the sub. They use **sonar**.

Ship Stats

USS *Nautilus*

Size	**323** feet (98.5 meters) long; **28** feet (8.5 meters) wide
Type	attack submarine
Top Speed	**23** knots (26 miles or 43 kilometers per hour)
Purpose	world's first nuclear-powered submarine

Attack subs have weapons. They are stored in the **torpedo** room.

Fire control **technicians** fire weapons. Computers help them know where to fire.

Officers fill and empty the sub's **ballast tanks**. The tanks help subs go underwater.

The tanks fill with water to sink. They fill with air to move up.

Moving Up and Down

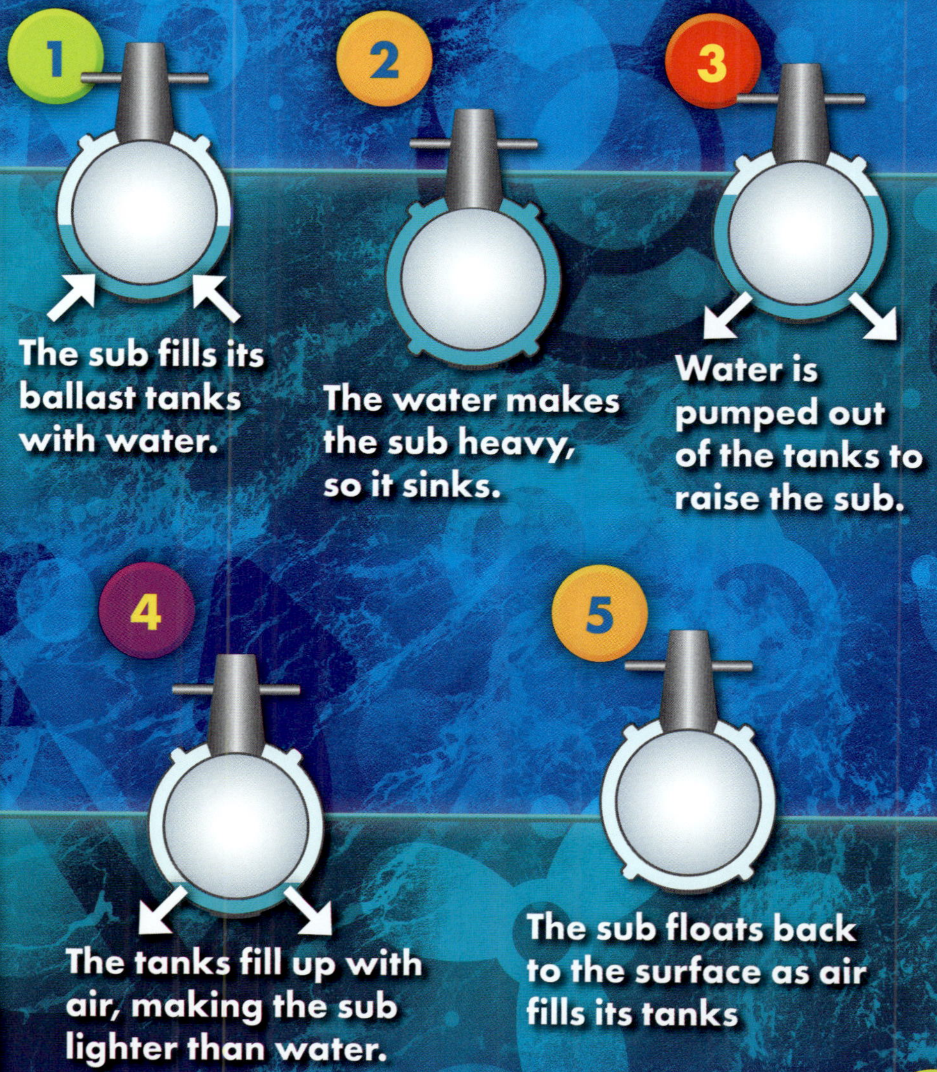

Some subs can reach speeds of more than 30 **knots** (35 miles or 56 kilometers per hour).

They can dive deep. Some can dive to around 1 mile (1.6 kilometers) underwater!

Working Underwater

Subs dive to dark ocean waters. Scientists use them to study plants and animals.

Submarines also help keep us safe. They are the heroes of the deep!

Glossary

ballast tanks—large parts on submarines that hold water or air

engine—related to machines with moving parts that change power into motion

knots—units of measurement used to explain the speed of a ship

nuclear reactor—a tool that helps create steam in order to provide energy to a ship

periscope—a long tube that sticks up from a sub's sail; the periscope is used to see above the surface of the water.

propeller—a spinning blade that helps a ship move

quartermaster—a person in charge of controlling where a submarine goes

research—related to collecting information about a subject in order to learn about it

sail—a towerlike part of a submarine that holds the periscope and other parts

sonar—a system that uses sound waves to find things underwater

steam—the gas that water turns into when it is heated

technicians—people whose job is to control a piece of equipment

torpedo—a tube-shaped weapon fired underwater

tour—related to learning about and seeing a place

To Learn More

AT THE LIBRARY

Humphrey, Natalie. *Super Submarines.* Buffalo, N.Y.: Gareth Stevens Publishing, 2023.

Lock, Deborah. *Submarines and Submersibles.* New York, N.Y.: DK, 2023.

Miller, Marie-Therese. *Strong Submarines.* Minneapolis, Minn.: Lerner Publications, 2025.

ON THE WEB

FACTSURFER

Factsurfer.com gives you a safe, fun way to find more information.

1. Go to www.factsurfer.com.
2. Enter "submarines" into the search box and click 🔍.
3. Select your book cover to see a list of related content.

Index

The images in this book are reproduced through the courtesy of: Aleksandr Merkushev, front cover; Aerial-motic pp. 3, 7, 11 (attack submarine); Stocktrek Images/ Getty Images, pp. 4-5, 10-11, 18-19; Mark Agnor, pp. 5, 11 (research submarine); Archaeonavall, pp. 6-7; Petty Officer 3rd Class Joshua Martin/ DVIDS, p. 7 (periscope); Eugene Sergeev/ Alamy Stock Photo, p. 7 (propellor); Kellie Randall/ DVIDS, p. 7 (nuclear reactor); Kostantinc Livadas/ Alamy Stock Photo, p. 8; Charles-Edouard Cote, pp. 8-9; Gino Santa Maria, p. 11 (tour submarine); Petty Officer 2nd Class David Negron/ DVIDS, pp. 12-13; PHC John Kristoffersen/ National Archives, p. 13; Lewis S. Parks Papers/ National Archives, p. 13 (inset); Petty Officer 2nd Class Jonathan Nelson/ DVIDS, pp. 14-15; Petty Officer 1st Class Nikita Custer/ DVIDS, p. 14 (torpedo); Lauren Laughlin/ DVIDS, p. 15; Seamc Joseph Weiser/ DVIDS, pp. 16-17; Stocktrek/ Getty Images, p. 19; Anton Petrus/ Getty Images, p. 20; Stepher Frink/ Getty Images, pp. 20-21; Birute Vijeikiene, p. 23.